How To Float

Tips and Tricks To Help Anyone Float When Learning How To Swim

Got that sinking feeling? Can't work out why some people float and while others sink?

Discover the facts about floating and sinking and learn some of the tricks to staying afloat from some simple exercises and top tips.

Published by: Educate & Learn Publishing, Hertfordshire, UK
ISBN: 978-0-9927428-8-1

Graphics by Mark Young, courtesy of Poser V6.0

Design and typeset by Mark Young

Published in association with swim-teach.com www.swim-teach.com

Author Online!

For help and advice with any part of this book, contact Mark Young at his website

www.swim-teach.com

Mark Young is a well-established swimming instructor with decades of experience, teaching thousands of adults and children to swim. He has taken nervous, frightened children and adults with a fear of water and made them happy, confident swimmers. He has also turned many of average ability into advanced swimmers. This book draws on his experiences and countless successes to put together this simplistic methodical approach to swimming.

Contents

Myths

Myth #1 - The harder and faster I kick, the more I will stay afloat.
Not true. Harder kicking almost always results in sinking.

Myth #2 - The faster I use my arms the more I will stay afloat.
Not true either. A faster arm action will not assist the body to stay up any more than a slower one.

Myth #3 - The water is trying to pull me down.
The water is in fact trying to support you.

Myth #4 - If I take a bigger breath and hold it for longer I will float.
A bigger inhalation of air is not enough to prevent your legs from sinking.

The Psychology Of Floating: What's going on in your head?

It is common in beginners and those with a fear of water to think that the water is pulling them down. As an adult learning to swim it is important to understand that the water is actually trying to support you.

The human body does not sink like a stone. Those of us that naturally sink, usually sink slowly and gradually.

So with that in mind, we have to move our arms and legs in a way that help the water to support us. Those movements can be very subtle, small ones or they may have to be larger movements to help generate some momentum.

Either way, most of us have to do our bit to help the water to support us. It is a matter of discovering our own level of buoyancy, which may not necessarily be at the water surface.

Why Do We Sink?

Floating is a characteristic of the human body. Some of us have good buoyancy while others do not. It is all down to our relative density. In other words, how dense our body structure is, compared to the density of the water we are attempting to float in.

Let us put some actual figures to this:
- Freshwater has a density of $1g/cm^3$
- Saltwater has a higher density of $1.024g/cm^3$

The average male has a density of $0.98g/cm^3$ and the average female $0.97g/cm^3$. We can deduce therefore that most human beings will float to a certain degree, with a small amount of the body staying above the water surface.

The diagram below shows our relative density compared to freshwater, which has a relative density of 1 gram per cubic centimetre ($1g/cm^3$).

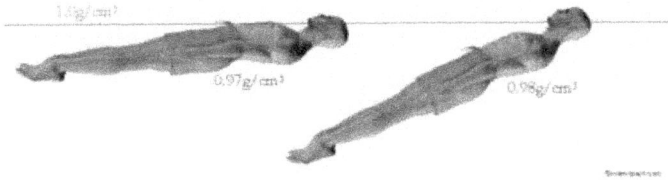

Generally speaking people that are muscular, lean or thin will tend to sink. Those that have a wider surface area or a larger body fat percentage will usually remain afloat for longer. That said, everybody's legs sink eventually due to their weight.

Do You Naturally Sink?

The simple facts are that fat floats and muscle sinks. Yes, fat people are better floaters than thin, or muscular people.
Generally speaking our legs are heavy and therefore sink and our upper body will tend to float because our lungs contain air.

But, the higher our body fat percentage the better chance we have of naturally staying afloat.

However, a person with low body fat percentage who is lean and has a higher density, can remain at the water surface as they swim. This is despite the fact their body naturally wants to sink.

Relax and Glide, Then Floating Becomes Easier

Feel your way through the water, don't fight your way through it. Learning how to relax in the pool will erase tension as you learn how your body moves and behaves in water.

A gliding action through the water as you swim is key to relaxing and the momentum of a glide helps to remain at the water surface and prevent sinking.

Moving through the water smoothly and with minimum effort is essential for the natural sinker to stay afloat.

Floating Stationary vs Floating As You Swim

Yes, there is a big difference. If you are not a natural floater, generally a lean or muscular person, then you will most likely sink as you remain stationary in the water. Our legs are heavy, and usually sink first

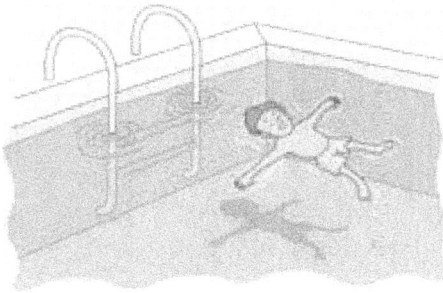

A poor floater can however remain at or near the water surface as they swim, providing they are relaxed and have some degree of swimming technique.

The propulsion gained from arm pulls and leg kicks generates momentum, which in turn aids in keeping a swimmer afloat as they move through the water.

Which Swimming Stroke Is Best For Staying Afloat?

Beginners learning to swim breaststroke will find floating easier than those learning to swim front crawl.

This is because the arm and leg movements of breaststroke are wider and therefore cover a larger surface area of water, making it easier to remain there.

The body position for breaststroke is angled so that the leg kick can occur slightly deeper under the water, favouring those of us that tend to sink.

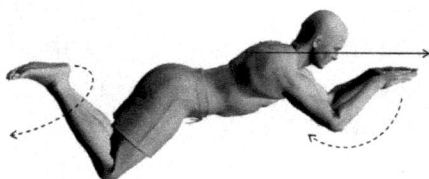

A powerful leg kick and correct timing and coordination are essential to preventing a breaststroke swimmer from sinking.

Front crawl however is a more streamlined stroke and therefore has a longer and more narrow shape. This makes it more difficult, especially for the legs, to stay up near the surface as they kick.

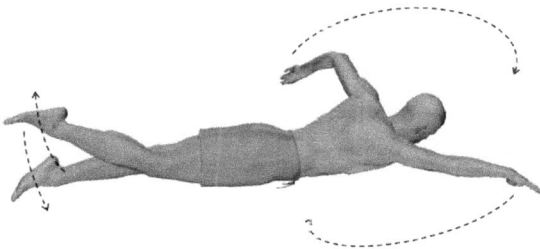

A relaxed and flowing front crawl leg kick is essential to keep the legs up near the surface. A faster, harder and more forceful kick will almost certainly result in the legs sinking quicker.

Front crawl relies on its arm action to generate most of its propulsion and movement.

How To Relax, Float And Be At One With The Water

Learning how to relax in the water and relax when swimming are vital components of learning how to swim.

Being 'at one' with the water helps to ensure that everything we do in the water and when we swim is second nature and therefore not stressful.

Essential elements of learning how to relax when swimming are:

- Learning how to breath hold and submerge
- Learn how to move through the water slowly
- Learn how to breathe regularly

Go Underwater and Really Experience It

Submerging completely under the water is a great way to learn how to relax. Grab a pair of swim goggles, put them on your eyes, take a deep breath and down you go.

What do you see? Everything very clearly, so you have a very clear perception of where you are and what you are doing.

What can you hear? Not much, if anything. All is peaceful and quiet.

Now try slowly moving about. Notice how gracefully you can move, almost like moving around on the moon without gravity. That is the water trying to support and lift you.

Obviously you can only do this for as long as you can hold your breath, but the more you do it, the more you get a feel for how your body behaves in the water.

As you get more of a feel for the water you will start to get an idea of your level of buoyancy. This means you can gradually work out how much or how little movement is required from your arms and legs to keep you at or near the water surface.

You don't actually have to do any swimming when you do this. Just go underwater and experiment. Play around. Get a feel for the water and eventually you become more comfortable and relaxed.

Slower Is Better

There is a common misconception in beginners learning how to swim, that the harder we kick, pull or paddle then the better our chances are of remaining at the water surface and actually swimming some distance. This is not true. Quite often the harder we kick, pull or paddle the less we move through the water and eventually we begin to sink.

The first rule of relaxing when we swim is to move slowly. Now you are thinking 'but if I move slowly I will sink'..? That is partly true, but if you move slowly you get a feel for the water and then begin to relax when swimming.

You must learn to 'feel' your way through the water and not 'fight' your way through it.

Get the concept into your head that the water is trying to support and hold you up. Beginners learning how to swim often think that the water is something that is trying to pull them down and that they have to fight to stay on top. This is particularly common in people that may have a fear of water or fear of swimming.

Water does not behave like that. Even those of us who do not float naturally and tend to sink, we sink very slowly and gradually. By moving our arms and legs in some kind of swimming manner, we are simply doing our bit to help the water to support us.

Breathe Before You Need To

Breathing regularly when we swim helps to keep us relaxed and calm.

It is very common to either hold our breath or exhale in the water, but do it to the point of exhaustion. The result being a frantic and panic stricken gasp for breath before submerging the face and repeating the pattern again.

So, breathe long before you need to. Don't wait for your breath to completely run out. Take a new breath at a point that is comfortable and easy to do. You wouldn't breathe out to the point of exhaustion when running or cycling, so why do it when you swim?

...And Relax

So you have become used to submerging underwater, you can move around with slow, gentle movements and you can breathe at comfortable moments when you need to. Everything you do in the water is now more relaxed. Your body is more relaxed.

Now apply these concepts and practices to your swimming technique and swim with a relaxed smooth stroke. You may be pleasantly surprised to find you can relax when swimming and do not sink anymore.

Gliding: The Missing Link To Relaxing And Floating

Learning how to glide when swimming is an important element of learning how to swim, how to relax in the water and how to float.

Gliding in aquatic terms is the concept of floating through the water, either at the surface or underwater, without assistance or movement from the arms or legs. It usually begins with a forceful push from the poolside or solid edge in order to generate some propulsion.

A streamlined body shape is important for a glide to gain and maintain some distance.

©swim-teach.com

Your personal 'body shape' is not relevant here. We are not talking about how short, tall, fat or thin you are. Any body shape can glide through the water. It is a matter of what position you have your arms and legs in as you glide.

Your hands and feet must be together to give a pointed streamlined shape so that the water moves easily around you as your body cuts through it. If your hands and feet are apart your body shape will be creating resistance and your movement will be little, if any.

Learning How To Glide When Swimming Can Be Scary

The thought of gliding through the water can be a scary one for a beginner learning to swim. That wobbly and unbalanced feeling as you move through the water unaided and without using your arms and legs, can be a very strange one.

Therefore it is important to start slowly. As you get used to the feeling of gliding you can push away harder and glide further. The more you repeat this, the more you getting used to how your body behaves in the water and this will then help to relax your body and mind.

Those of us that are not natural floaters will begin to discover the point at which we sink, as our glide begins to slow. We can also learn how fast we sink, which in reality is actually very slow no matter how heavy we are.

As our glide slows and we begin to sink, we can apply some basic movements to help maintain the glide and prevent us sinking.

Combine your relaxed glide through the water with some gentle but effective arm and leg movements and you will soon discover that you float and remain at the surface as you swim.

Breathing: The Crucial Link Between Relaxing And Floating

What is wrong with my swimming breathing? Probably the most commonly asked question to a swimming teacher and coach.
There are a few points to consider and tips to try out in the pool to help make your breathing easier as you swim...

It all comes down to how to breathe, when to breathe and how often to breathe. All of which will depend on which stroke you are swimming.

The breathing technique for front crawl is slightly different to the breathing technique for breaststroke. However there are some similarities too, and common mistakes.

The 2 most common swimming breathing mistakes

When it comes to breathing during swimming, whichever swimming stroke you are attempting to swim, there are two common mistakes that many adults make:

- Holding the breath
- Breathing too late

Do Not Hold Your Breath!

Firstly we hold our breath, even though we think we are breathing out into the water. Our breath is held instinctively without knowing it. Therefore when it comes to taking a breath we have to breathe out and in again in the short split second our mouth is out of the water. This is too short a time to take a controlled breath and usually results in a mouth full of water.

Also, holding our breath causes a rapid increase in carbon dioxide in our respiratory system.

This in turn increases the urgency to breathe again because carbon dioxide is a waste product that needs to be exhaled. The net result is more frequent and rapid breaths. Not good when you're trying to relax and swim.

The solution is to ensure you are breathing out into the water as you swim. Breathe out in a slow controlled way without forcing the air out so that when you turn your head to breathe in again, inhaling is all you need to do and you have plenty of time to do it comfortably.

Breathe Before You Need To

The second most common mistake it to leave it right to the last second to take a breath. In other words we wait until all oxygen has completely expired and we are almost gasping for air. We turn our head to breathe and the action becomes a rushed panic, also resulting in a mouth full of water.

The solution here is to breath long before you need to.

BREATH IN

BREATH OUT
©swim-teach.com

breathing technique for front crawl
Set yourself a certain number of arm pulls (3 or 4 is usually most comfortable for front crawl)

and breathe at that set point. The breathing pattern will change as you become more tired over time, but at least your breathing should be easier.

Combine breathing out into the water in a slow, controlled way with taking breaths early.

Providing your swimming overall is relaxed and smooth and you have decent technique, you should find yourself swimming longer distance and becoming less out of breath.

That is the theory of easier swimming breathing and it will of course take practice and time.

What actually happens when you hold your breath?

Breath holding is an unnatural act for a human being to carry out. That is why some people find it difficult and even stressful.

The human body has several responses to breath holding and some additional responses to being submerged in water. It is how we deal with these responses that determine how comfortable or uncomfortable we are and therefore what duration of time we are able to spend underwater whilst holding our breath.

Firstly, the amount of air we are able to inhale into our lungs depends on the size of our lungs. It may seem obvious but a taller person will have larger lungs, and therefore will be able fill them with more oxygen and remain underwater for longer.

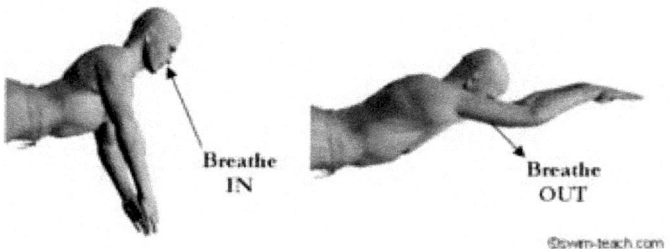

Breathe
IN

Breathe
OUT

©swim-teach.com

breathing technique for breaststroke

Whilst we are holding our breath, the amount of oxygen in our lungs decreases as it is carried away in the blood stream and used, and the amount of carbon dioxide increases.

Carbon dioxide is a waste product and when a certain level is reached a signal is sent to the brain to tell you to breath again.

Changes in heart rate occur whilst breath holding and the more relaxed a person is, the slower they consume oxygen and therefore the longer they can remain holding their breath.

Submerging under the water brings about its own stresses, especially for a beginner learning swimming breathing.

The experience can be made easier by wearing goggles or a mask so that the eyes can remain open, giving the person an awareness of their surroundings and therefore keeping them in a relaxed state.

Relaxing is the key to swimming breathing

Relaxation underwater is governed mainly by a slow heart rate. As heart rate increases so does oxygen consumption and therefore levels of stress and anxiety. Movement of any part of the body will increase heart rate and with it oxygen consumption.

Holding our breath underwater is made easier by slowly breathing out short bursts of air. This expels carbon dioxide, reducing the amount present in the lungs. This then delays the trigger to breath.

Exercises To Help Discover Your Level Of Buoyancy And Stay Afloat

All of the exercises listed below are designed to help discover your own level of buoyancy and if you are a natural sinker, how fast or slow you actually sink.

Providing you have read the previous parts of this book that explain how to relax, how to glide and how to breathe, you can then use these exercises to help keep your body up and keep it moving.

Wearing swim goggles will help to give you a greater sense of awareness.

Exercise #1: Face Down Floating

Take a deep breath and submerge your face whilst bringing your legs up to the surface. Lay face down with arms and legs wide to cover as much surface area as possible. Lay there for as long as you can hold your breath and feel how your body behaves in this stationary position.

You will most probably find your legs slowly sinking first. See how slowly they sink and if there are any small movements that can slow down their rate of sinking or even help them back to the surface.

Maybe perform a very slow breaststroke, feeling your way through the water.

Exercise #2: Push and Glide

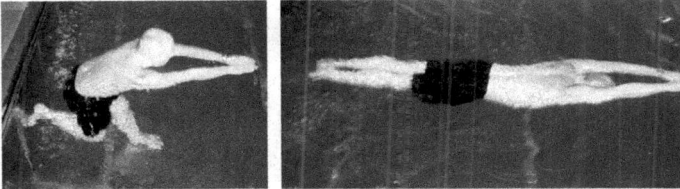

Take a deep breath and push away from the pool wall, face down. Ensure your body is in a stretched out, streamlined position. Glide as far as you can in one breath.

You may find you begin to sink as your momentum slows. See what small movements of the legs, feet and hands are able to keep you moving and afloat.

Feel your way through the water using a gentle breaststroke or front crawl action.

Exercise #3: Push and Glide With Kicks

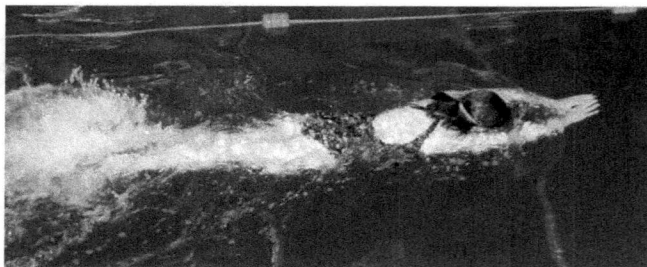

The same exercise as #2 with a push and glide from the poolside. This time add leg kicks to help maintain the momentum and prevent sinking.

The leg kicks can be an alternating kick such the kick used in front crawl, or a simultaneous circular leg kick like the one used for breaststroke.

Exercise #4: Push and Glide On The Back

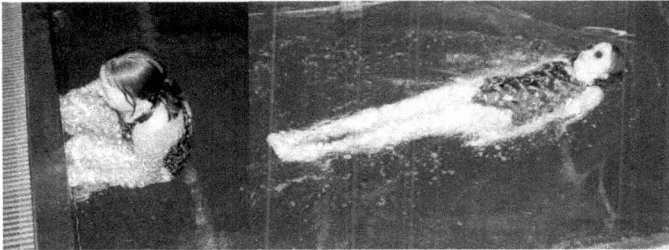

Perform a push and glide from the poolside in a supine (face up) position. Ensure your head is looking upwards and chest and hips are high up near the water surface. This will help enable the legs and feet to be at or near the water surface too.

As the glide begins to slow, use the hands by the sides in a sculling type action (using the wrists to help the hands push water towards the feet) under the water and a gentle leg kick to maintain the movement and momentum through the water.

Tips and Tricks

Tip #1
When swimming face up on your front and your legs begin to sink, take a deep breath and put your face down in the water. The act of putting your face into the water will, with some assistance from yourself encourage your legs to rise again.

Tip #2
When swimming breaststroke use a slightly downward arm pull action. Although breaststroke arm pull is a circular action to help pull through the water, a downwards pull with help to pull the body upwards in the water. This also assists us to breathe as the upper body rises.

Tip #3
Slow down. Swimming slower encourages relaxation, a gliding action and gives us time to breathe, all of which assist us in remaining at the water surface.

Tip #4
Feel your way through the water, don't fight your way through it. Fight the water and it will usually win. Feel you way through it and you will be doing your bit to help the water to support you.

Correct Technique Is The Key

Staying afloat as we swim is all about making our body as efficient as possible as we move through the water. Our body has to cut its way through the water and correct swimming technique is essential for this to happen.

The finer details of the techniques required for each of the swimming strokes are beyond the realms of this short book about how to float.

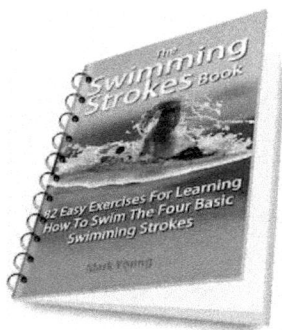

However everything you need to know is contained in '**The Swimming Strokes Book**', also by Mark Young

82 exercises covering each separate stroke will help you to perform and perfect each of the four basic swimming strokes.

Visit Swim Teach (www.swim-teach.com) to find out more.

More books by Mark Young:

The Complete Guide To Simple Swimming
Everything You Need to Know from Your First Entry
into the Pool to Swimming the Four Basic Strokes

The Swimming Strokes Book:
82 Easy Exercises For Learning How To Swim The
Four Basic Swimming Strokes

How To Be A Swimming Teacher
The Definitive Guide To Becoming A Successful
Swimming Teacher

How To Swim Front Crawl
A Step-By-Step Guide For Beginners Learning Front
Crawl Technique

How To Swim Breaststroke
A Step-By-Step Guide For Beginners Learning
Breaststroke Technique

How To Swim Backstroke
A Step-By-Step Guide For Beginners Learning
Backstroke Technique

How To Swim Butterfly
A Step-By-Step Guide For Beginners Learning
Butterfly Technique